A Midsummer Night's Dream

A PRACTICAL GUIDE FOR TEACHING SHAKESPEARE IN THE MIDDLE GRADE CLASSROOM

Retold by Alain Chirinian

Illustrated by Robin DeWitt & Patricia Grush

Project Director: Mina McMullin

Senior Editor: Christine Hood

Inside and Cover Design: Rita Hudson

Cover Illustration: Robin DeWitt

 GOOD APPLE
A Division of Frank Schaffer Publications
23740 Hawthorne Blvd.
Torrance, CA 90505

Contents

Introduction

If you asked 100 people to name the greatest writer in history, most of them would probably say, *William Shakespeare*. Shakespeare, a cultural icon of the English-speaking world, has been revered throughout history for his extraordinary skill with language; his unforgettable characters; and his wonderful, many-faceted stories. Some people have been led to believe that Shakespeare is difficult to understand or just not relevant to today's world. Unfortunately, many students' first exposure to Shakespeare may be sitting in a classroom passively listening to the teacher lecture or analyzing passages that seem to have no meaning or relevance to their lives. Studying Shakespeare should not be a "passive" experience; rather, it should be exciting, stimulating, and most of all, fun! It is for this reason that this book was created.

When students are drawn into the humanity of Shakespeare's work, they see how it relates to their lives and the world around them. His themes are central to the struggles and triumphs of humankind; his characters highlight the strength, passion, and joy of humanity as well as its darker, more malevolent side. Although the settings of his stories are in faraway times and places, they deal with contemporary topics. Shakespeare wrote of people in the depths of despair, the throes of comic madness, diabolical plotting, scheming, wooing, and "lovemaking." This may sound like the stuff of soap operas, movies, or TV sitcoms, but that is exactly why students will relate to Shakespeare—a writer for all ages.

In order for students to truly enjoy and appreciate Shakespeare, they shouldn't just read his work, but rather, "experience" it. Before beginning a play study, introduce Shakespeare as a person. Where was he born? What do we know about his life? his family? What was England like during Shakespeare's time? Were his plays as popular then as they are today? What was the life of an actor and playwright like in Elizabethan England? Answering these and other questions for students gives them a personal and historical perspective on Shakespeare and the Elizabethan stage, complementing their overall understanding and enjoyment of his plays.

This book contains a simple summary and an edited version of the play *A Midsummer Night's Dream*, in which some language has been simplified for easier student understanding. It also provides suggestions for performing the play; a comprehensive vocabulary list; journal/discussion topics; and a myriad of activities that draw students into the plot, characters, and meaning of the story. These activities will help develop children's imaginations; language and critical-thinking skills; and creative expression through writing, dramatic presentation, and art.

If students' first encounter with Shakespeare is a positive one, they will be "turned on" to future experiences. Learning that "old" doesn't necessarily mean "old-fashioned" opens not only Shakespeare's world to students, but also that of other classic writers and artists.

The Life and Times of William Shakespeare

Shakespeare's plays do not reveal much about him as a person. Since the plots are so varied and deal with a myriad of social and political issues, Shakespeare's actual views remain elusive and mysterious.

Shakespeare's birthday is recognized as April 23, 1564. He was born in the small English town of Stratford-upon-Avon. The town's name developed because Stratford was nestled next to the River Avon. Shakespeare's father, John, was a successful Stratford glove maker who dealt in leather goods; and his mother, Mary Arden, came from a wealthy Catholic family.

Not much is known about Shakespeare until his marriage to Anne Hathaway in 1582. He was 18 and she was 26. During their marriage, they had three children—Susanna, born in 1583, and the twins Judith and Hamnet, born in 1585.

From 1585 to 1592, no official records exist on Shakespeare. But by the age of 28, he had moved to London and become an actor with a small company of players. Even as he became a successful playwright, he continued to act in his own and others' plays. Between 1589 and 1594, Shakespeare's first plays, *Henry VI*, *Titus Andronicus*, and *The Comedy of Errors*, were a huge success in the London theatre circuit. Shakespeare soon made a name for himself and attained instant popularity.

London was a very exciting place during Shakespeare's time. Elizabeth I was queen when he began his career. English ships ruled the seas, and English explorers were claiming territories as far away as America and the Far East. Shakespeare incorporated much of the excitement, mystery, and adventure of this time period into his work. Unfortunately, in the early 1590s, the plague in London led to the closing of all the theatres. During this time, Shakespeare began writing poetry, including his famous sonnets. This poetry demonstrates Shakespeare's true artistic skill with verse.

When the theatres reopened around 1594, Shakespeare helped form the acting company known as the Lord Chamberlain's Men. For the next ten years, it was London's most popular acting company. The company also started its own theater—the Globe—and Shakespeare became the primary shareholder. The Globe became a popular entertainment spot for both commoners and wealthy aristocrats.

Shakespeare's greatest writing occurred between 1599 and 1608. During this time, he wrote such popular plays as *Twelfth Night*, *Hamlet*, *Macbeth*, and *Othello*. In 1603, with the succession of James I, Shakespeare's company received a royal patent, and they changed their name to the King's Men. They were then able to perform at the royal court several times a year.

Between 1610 and 1611, Shakespeare retired to his home in Stratford. Here he collaborated with John Fletcher on three more plays—*Henry VIII*, *The Two Noble Kinsmen*, and *Cardenio*.

In 1616, Shakespeare died at the young age of 52. Records show that he was buried on April 25, so it's assumed he died on April 23, two days earlier. This date has been suspect since it is also his birthday. No one knows how Shakespeare died, so his death remains shrouded in mystery. Over 20 possible causes of death have been speculated, including writer's cramp, too much alcohol, and murder.

Regardless of what brought Shakespeare to his demise, his incredible life left humankind a prolific treasure in his writings. Shakespeare wrote 37 plays, 154 sonnets, and two narrative poems. His plays fall into three categories: histories such as *Richard III* and *Henry V*, tragedies such as *Macbeth* and *Othello*, and comedies such as *Twelfth Night* and *As You Like It*.

Shakespeare's deep understanding of human nature and his incredible talent for making characters realistic and human make his work uniquely great. Most aspects of human nature haven't changed much from Elizabethan England. One may even find something of him- or herself or a friend in one of Shakespeare's characters. Much as they did in Elizabethan England, these plays can still move audiences to tears or make them roar with laughter. It is these timeless qualities that keep Shakespeare at the top of the literary and theatrical world.

The Elizabethan Stage

Theatre was an entirely different experience for the Elizabethans than it is for audiences today. The stage was round, so the audience was highly involved in the performance. Actors sometimes spoke to the audience through soliloquies and asides, and audience members often answered back. Elizabethan theatregoers yelled, laughed, taunted, talked, and ate throughout the performance.

During the Elizabethan period, politicians and clergy were opposed to the theatre, claiming it was a dangerous diversion from religion. So, playhouses were banned in London's city proper and forced out to the suburbs in an area known as Southwark. In this "theatre district," patrons could choose between nine different theatres. Strewn among the theatres were pubs, taverns, and bawdy houses as well as pickpockets and thieves, which only added to the theatre's already bad reputation.

When a play was about to begin, it was announced with a raised flag and a trumpeted fanfare. The flag indicated the theme of that day's play—black for tragedy, white for comedy, and red for history. When patrons entered a theatre for a performance, they placed their admission money in a box (or "box office"). They could sit in the "galleries" on wooden benches, on cushions in front of the stage, on the stage itself (for more money), or stand in back with the crowd. The general "mob scene" of the crowd (known as "groundlings") created quite a spectacle. Since few Elizabethans bathed, the theatres smelled of sweat, beer, and garlic. It's no wonder the groundlings were also referred to as "penny stinkards."

Vendors sold beer, fruit, and nuts, and in the often tumultuous, rowdy atmosphere of a play, these snacks would sometimes be thrown at the actors onstage.

Like all other playhouses, Shakespeare's Globe was under the patronage of a nobleman. This patronage provided protection from the Puritans as well as additional financial backing. Shakespeare's company was originally "attached" to Lord Chamberlain, and later to James I, becoming the most prestigious theatre company in London.

Shakespeare wrote specifically for his stage in the Globe. Often referred to as a "wooden O," the Globe may have had as many as 20 sides to provide its circular appearance. The theatre was open to the outside and could hold close to 3,000 people. The stage consisted of three tiers—"heaven," "earth," and "hell." A trapdoor in the main stage, or "earth," was used to raise and lower actors and props into and out of "hell." A canopy over the stage was painted with golden stars to represent the "heavens." Often, pulleys and ropes lowered or "whisked" actors up to and from "heaven." A hut on top of the canopy housed props for sound effects such as thunder and cannon fire. Audiences hooted and hollered with delight when such special stage and sound effects were used.

Unlike plays and movies today, scenery and props were limited. To let the audience know what time of day it was or what the weather was like, it was described with an actor's words. For example, when Romeo and Juliet awaken in her chamber, we know it is morning when Romeo says, "It was the lark, the herald of the morn . . . Look, love, what envious streaks do lace the severing clouds in yonder east." Actors also wore elaborate, gawdy costumes and makeup, which were considered sinful by the clergy.

During this time, women were not allowed to act on the public stage, so young boys played the female roles. That is one reason why there are so few women characters in Shakespeare's plays. Not being able to rely on "traditional" feminine beauty for his female characters, Shakespeare created those with amazing intelligence and wit.

Theatres put on a great variety of plays every season. In six months, one company might give about 150 performances of 25 to 30 different plays. Given the quick turnover, rehearsal time was extremely short. Actors only had about a week to learn their parts—up to 800 lines a day for leading roles!

Unfortunately, Shakespeare's revered Globe Theatre burned down in 1613 during a performance of *Henry VIII*. A prop cannon exploded and set the theatre aflame. The theatre was eventually rebuilt, but in 1642, the Puritans finally got their way. The English Parliament passed an ordinance shutting down all the theatres, and as a result, the Globe was destroyed in 1644.

About
A Midsummer Night's Dream

"Love looks not with the eyes, but with the mind." These words, spoken by Helena in *A Midsummer Night's Dream*, represent this play's major theme. At this point in the play, the young Athenian, Helena, is in love with Demetrius, who is in love with Helena's best friend Hermia. Helena knows she is as beautiful as Hermia, but that Demetrius' love for her friend is not based on beauty, but on how he *thinks* about her. In this fanciful dreamscape, Shakespeare demonstrates how love is a form of enchantment, or "spell." He throws together a delightful cast of characters, ranging from commoners, to dukes and ladies, to the king and queen of fairies. The surreal, supernatural wood in which most of the story takes place brings together all levels of society. Love, in its most blinding form, crosses all lines. Traditional societal distinctions blur or disappear altogether, and the ordinary is transformed into the extraordinary. Stereotypical, almost interchangeable lovers Helena, Hermia, Lysander, and Demetrius are transformed to unique individuals under the mysterious powers of love. Helena wisely realizes, "Things base and vile, holding no quantity, love can transpose to form and dignity."

The fairies in this play have great fun playing with the affections of the "mortals" as delightful love mix-ups occur. But the fairy world is not immune to chaos. King of the fairies, Oberon, lets jealousy drive him to place a spell on his own wife, causing her to fall in love with one of the "lowest" characters in the story. This coupling demonstrates how reason has truly been turned on its head, and reveals the tenuous boundary between reality and dreams, reason and insanity.

After order has been restored, the lovers awaken as if from a dream, and no one is the wiser except the sprite Puck, who joyfully mocks the mortals. From his superior perspective, the mortal world appears ridiculous, just as the "actors" appear ridiculous to the aristocrats at the story's end. It is this "play within a play" mirror image that connects each level of the story—the supernatural world, the aristocratic world, and the world of commoners. Outside the wood, these worlds are separated by status and class. But within the wood, these worlds not only combine, but also share common elements. No one is immune to chaos or absurdity.

Much of this play seems dreamlike, and many of it's characters as if they are sleepwalking. Though everything ends up as it should, and lovers are successfully matched, no one seems quite sure how it all happened. Ironically, it is Bottom who realizes, "I have had a most rare vision. I have had a dream, past the wit of man to say what dream it was. Man is but an ass if he go about to expound on his dream."

A Midsummer Night's Dream
Summary

The story takes place in ancient Athens, a place of tradition, grandeur, and culture. Within its walls lives a duke and duchess, the educated and uneducated, the rich and the poor. It is a place where boundaries of status and class separate its citizens. Outside Athens' walls exists a wood, rich with magic, mystery, and enchantment. Here, boundaries seem vague, and life, surreal, as if one were walking into a dream . . .

❧ ACT ONE ❧

Theseus, Duke of Athens, and Hippolyta, his bride to be, are making plans for their wedding day when Egeus, one of the duke's royal subjects, comes to visit. He is unhappy because his daughter Hermia will not agree to marry Demetrius, the man to whom she is promised. "I have promised my daughter to Demetrius," Egeus tells the duke. "And she refuses to obey my wishes." Hermia tells the duke she can't marry Demetrius because she is in love with another man.

But it doesn't matter. The duke informs Hermia that she has to obey her father's wishes. She has three choices—marry Demetrius, be put to death, or live in a convent as a nun. She has four days to make her decision. Hermia is devastated with the news.

Afterward, Lysander, the man Hermia loves, comes to her with a plan. He and Hermia will secretly steal away the next night and travel through the forest away from Athens. Their journey will take them to another city where they can marry legally.

Helena, Hermia's best friend, is heart-broken over the situation, for she is in love with Demetrius. She wishes she were marrying him instead of Hermia, but Demetrius loves Hermia. Hermia and Lysander tell Helena of their plan to escape the following night, and swear her to secrecy. Unfortunately for Hermia and Lysander, Helena does not keep their secret. She decides to tell Demetrius of their plan, hoping he will be so thankful that he will reject Hermia and love her instead.

Meanwhile, a troupe of part-time actors meet to learn about their next play. Peter Quince, the writer of the play, assigns everyone to a part. The play will be called *The Most Lamentable Comedy, and Most Cruel Death of Pyramus and Thisby*. Nick Bottom is happy to hear he will be the star of the play, Pyramus. Francis Flute will play the role of Thisby. Flute begs Quince not to make him play a woman, but Quince insists. "You shall wear a mask to hide your face," Quince tells him. Quince quickly assigns the other roles in the play to the remaining actors. Snug will play the lion; Starveling, Thisby's mother; Snout, Pyramus' father; and himself, Thisby's father. Everyone worries that the "lion" will frighten the ladies in the audience. That would mean a trip to jail or even death for the actors! Nevertheless, rehearsal for the play is scheduled for the following night in the woods, so no one will be able to see the play before the duke and his wedding guests.

⚜ ACT TWO ⚜

In the very same woods that night, Puck, a lively sprite, meets with a fairy. This fairy is an attendant to Titania, queen of the fairies. Puck is known throughout the forest as a creator of great mischief among mortals. Many tales have been told of how he causes stools to break under old women as they sit, turns milk sour, and snaps at gossips like a crab. "Be certain Titania does not encounter king Oberon tonight," he tells the fairy. "Oberon is very angry with her." Oberon, king of the fairies, wants a child Titania has taken from an Indian king. The child belonged to a friend of Titania's who died in childbirth. King Oberon thought the child would make an excellent personal attendant, and when Titania refused to give up the child, Oberon became extremely upset.

Soon after, as Puck and the fairy look on, Oberon and Titania meet in the forest clearing. Again Oberon asks Titania for the child, and again she refuses. After Titania leaves with her train, Oberon decides to punish her for her insolence, and devises a plan.

"Find the flower with the juice that makes a person, upon awakening, fall in love with the first living thing seen," he tells Puck. He then sends Puck on a mission to find the flower and bring it back to him.

The moment Puck leaves, Demetrius and Helena stumble into the clearing. Oberon stays behind to watch them. Demetrius is searching for Hermia and Lysander, having heard from Helena that they escaped into the forest that night. Helena persistently follows him. "I do not love you, so stop following me," Demetrius tells her. Helena proclaims she can't live without him. "Very well," Demetrius replies. "I will leave you alone in the woods." He leaves her alone in the darkness, and though Helena tries to follow, she is unable to keep up.

Seeing this, Oberon feels disgusted with Demetrius' behavior and decides to get involved in the lives of these two young Athenians. When Puck returns with the flower, Oberon instructs him to take some of the flower juice and place it on the eyes of a man wearing Athenian clothing. The juice should only be placed on the man's eyes when Puck is sure he will see Helena when he first wakes up, thereby falling in love with her.

Oberon sends Puck on his way, and then goes in search of Titania. He finds Titania asleep on a bed of flowers. He carefully squeezes some of the flower juice on her eyelids, and then disappears.

Meanwhile, Lysander and Hermia have become lost in the woods. They decide to rest and continue their journey in the morning. Puck comes upon the two sleeping Athenians, and places the flower juice on the Lysander's eyelids, mistaking him for Demetrius. Both men are wearing Athenian clothing, so Puck is none the wiser.

In another part of the woods, Hermia tires of trying to keep up with Demetrius and decides to try and find her way home. Suddenly, she comes upon the sleeping Lysander and Hermia. Helena wakes Lysander, and since she is the first living thing he lays eyes on, he falls madly in love with her. "Through fire I will run for thy sweet sake," he proclaims. Shocked and bewildered, Helena believes Lysander mocks her as some cruel joke. She knows he is really in love with Hermia, and she storms off angrily. Lysander runs after her.

Hermia then awakens to find her Lysander gone. She has been having a bad nightmare, and is desperate for his comfort. She gets up and decides to try and find him.

⚜ ACT THREE ⚜

In the woods near where Titania lies asleep, the acting troupe begins rehearsal. They decide the roaring lion will be too ferocious for the ladies in the audience, so the actor will explain he is not really a lion, but a man dressed as a lion.

Puck comes upon the rehearsing group and watches for a few moments, imagining what sort of mischief he might cause. Aha! As Nick Bottom comes in to say his part, Puck changes his head into that of a donkey. Upon seeing this, Peter Quince cries, "O monstrous! O strange! We are haunted. Help!" The actors run away from Bottom and his donkey head, much to Puck's amusement.

Imagining his friends are playing a mean joke on him, Bottom begins to sing so they won't think he is afraid of being in the forest alone. Titania awakens at the sound of his singing, and falls instantly in love. The queen of the fairies summons her attendants to fawn over Bottom, feeding him, scratching him behind his long ears, and making him ever so comfortable.

Puck returns to Oberon to tell him of his excellent work. As they speak, Demetrius and Hermia appear. Hermia ran into Demetrius in her search for Lysander, and now he will not leave her alone. Demetrius professes his love for Hermia, just as before. But Hermia is convinced that Demetrius has harmed Lysander. She curses him, demanding Lysander be returned. Demetrius insists he hasn't even seen Lysander, but Hermia runs away, determined to find her love. Demetrius, growing weary of the chase, lies down and falls asleep.

After observing this scene, Oberon is furious with Puck. "What hast thou done?" he demands. "You have laid the potion on the wrong man. It was this Athenian on whom you were to place the flower juice!" Puck tells Oberon it is an honest mistake, since both men are wearing Athenian clothing.

"Go find Helena," Oberon instructs him. "In the meantime, I will place the potion on the sleeping Demetrius' eyes, and be sure that Helena is the first person he sees when he wakes up!"

Soon Helena and Lysander wander by where Demetrius sleeps. Helena wants nothing to do with Lysander, and still searches for Demetrius, whom she loves. Demetrius wakes up when he hears them, and upon seeing Helena, falls instantly in love with her. "O Helena, goddess, nymph, perfect, divine!" he cries.

Helena is shocked. She can hardly believe Demetrius is being truthful, and is sure he and Lysander are playing a cruel joke on her. "What about Hermia?" Lysander asks Demetrius. "I thought you loved her."

"My love for Hermia is melted as the snow," Demetrius replies. "I love Helena."

Hermia shows up moments later only to find that Lysander is no longer in love with her, but with Helena! Both she and Helena are shocked and amazed. Now Helena believes Lysander, Demetrius, and her best friend Hermia are all trying to make a fool out of her. Demetrius and Lysander agree to fight to the death to see who will win Helena's heart, and they leave for a better spot to duel. Helena and Hermia argue and accuse each other, and eventually part ways as bitter enemies.

Hoping to correct the confusion, Oberon commands Puck to cause a great fog to fall over the forest, so the two men cannot find each other and fight. Calling to each other, Lysander and Demetrius are separated further and further by Puck's tricks. Soon, Lysander and Demetrius both tire and fall asleep.

Meanwhile, Helena, looking for a way back to Athens, and Hermia, searching for Lysander, also lie down and fall asleep. Now that all four Athenians are asleep, Puck applies the flower juice to Lysander's eyes so he will again be in love with Hermia.

❧ ACT FOUR ❧

In another part of the woods, Nick Bottom is enjoying his treatment by queen Titania and her servants. He orders them around, has them bring food, sing to him, and of course, scratch behind his large ears. However, all the activity tires Bottom, and he falls asleep in Titania's arms.

Observing this, Oberon is delighted with the results of his scheme. He has punished Titania well enough for refusing to give him the young child, and in her strange state, she has agreed to give him the boy. Now Oberon begins to feel sorry for his wife and decides it is time to end the spell. As Titania sleeps, Oberon applies the flower juice to her eyes, and then awakens her.

"Oberon!" the queen cries. "I had visions that I was in love with an ass."

"There lies your love," says Oberon, pointing to Bottom.

"Oh, how disgusting!" Titania exclaims. "How did this happen?"

"Never mind," Oberon replies, comforting her. "Now Puck, replace this man's head, and let us celebrate!"

The wedding day of Theseus and Hippolyta has now arrived. Theseus calls for a hunt to find a large animal to roast at the feast. As Theseus, Hippolyta, and their friend Egeus walk toward the hunting grounds, they come upon the four sleeping Athenians—Hermia, Lysander, Helena, and Demetrius. Hearing noises, they wake up, surprised and startled.

"Isn't this the day Hermia must decide her fate, whether she will marry Demetrius as you commanded her, be put to death, or live in a nunnery?" asks Theseus.

"It is," Egeus replies.

The duke asks the young men how they came together in the forest since they are bitter enemies. The four young Athenians seem confused and groggy, and have no answers to his questions. Egeus asks for the law to come down on Lysander's head for trying to escape with his daughter Hermia. But Demetrius protests, claiming he now loves Helena and no longer wants to marry Hermia.

The duke is delighted that everyone seems to be getting along, and proclaims that Hermia no longer has to marry Demetrius, since he is happily in love with another woman. "Egeus," the duke proclaims, "there shall indeed be a wedding as you had planned, but it shall be sooner than later. For in the temple by and by with us shall these couples be wed. Now, let us return to Athens for a feast."

After the duke and his train leave, the four young Athenians stand alone for a few moments. They are confused, and none of them quite remember what happened the night before. It's as though it was all a dream. Pondering these thoughts, they make their way to the temple.

When Bottom wakes up, he imagines for a moment that he is still rehearsing for the play. "Most fair Pyramus," he recites, half asleep. "Wait a moment! Where is everyone? I though I was . . . but then I was . . . Oh, it must have been a dream. And what a dream it was! Man is but an ass if he go about to expound on his dream!"

Back at Quince's house, the other actors worry about Bottom. "Without him, the play is doomed," Quince exclaims. Just then, Bottom enters the room, changed back to his human form. The other actors want to know what happened, but Bottom insists they hurry to the duke's palace to perform their play.

❧ ACT FIVE ❧

At the palace, Philostrate, Theseus' entertainment advisor, informs Theseus about the play. Philostrate tells him the actors are amateurs, and the play is very simple. Perhaps they should forget the play and enjoy other entertainment instead, he suggests. "I will hear that play," Theseus insists. "For never can anything be amiss, when simpleness and duty tender it."

As the play unfolds, the duke, his wife, and the four young Athenians poke fun at the ridiculous dramatics displayed before them. The play is a tragedy about Pyramus and Thisby, two lovers separated by a wall. When kissing through a crack in the wall doesn't work, they agree to meet that night at a family tomb. Unfortunately, an unfriendly lion chases Thisby away from the tomb before Pyramus arrives. Pyramus, upon seeing Thisby's bloodied cape, assumes she is dead, and kills himself. Thisby, having escaped the lion, returns to find her Pyramus dead at the tomb. She then kills herself as well.

As the play comes to an end, Bottom asks if he should provide an epilogue. Theseus can take the melodramatics no longer and kindly tells Bottom to forget the epilogue, because it is late and time for bed. As everyone goes off to their bedrooms, the fairies gather together in the palace. Titania blesses the newly-married couples, and the fairies stray throughout the house to tend to the dreams of the lovers.

CAST OF CHARACTERS

Theseus Duke of Athens

Hippolyta Queen of the Amazons, engaged to Theseus

Egeus Father of Hermia

Demetrius In love with Hermia

Lysander In love with Hermia

Philostrate Theseus' entertainment advisor

Hermia Daughter of Egeus, in love with Lysander

Helena In love with Demetrius

Quince a Carpenter

Snug a Joiner

Bottom a Weaver

Flute a Bellows-Mender

Snout a Tinker

Starveling a Tailor

Oberon King of the fairies

Titania Queen of the fairies

Puck a Sprite, also known as Robin Goodfellow

Peaseblossom, Cobweb, Moth, Mustardseed Fairies

Other fairies attending their king and queen

Attendants to Theseus and Hippolyta

A Midsummer Night's Dream
Setting

This story begins in Classical Greece, in the city of Athens. It then moves to an enchanted wood on the city's outskirts. Here, surrounded by fairies and sprites, the structured lives of the Athenians become surreal and magical.

❦ ACT ONE ❦

SCENE ONE *The city of Athens. A room in the palace of Theseus.*

Enter Theseus, Hippolyta, Philostrate, and attendants.

Theseus Four days, Hippolyta, four more days! The new moon then brings us a our wedding. The time cannot pass fast enough.

Hippolyta Four days will quickly become nights; four nights will quickly dream away the time.

Theseus Hippolyta, I woo'd thee with my sword, and won thy love. But now I will wed thee with festivities and merriment.

Enter Egeus, Hermia, Lysander, and Demetrius.

Egeus Happy be Theseus, our renowned duke!

Theseus Thanks, good Egeus. What's the news with thee?

Egeus Full of vexation I come, with complaint against my daughter Hermia. Stand forth, Demetrius. *(Demetrius moves forward.)* My noble lord, this man has my consent to marry Hermia. Stand forth, Lysander. *(Lysander moves forward.)* This man has bewitched the heart of my daughter, and she has fallen in love with him. He has tricked her with trinkets and baubles, bracelets and sweetmeats. Lysander turned her obedience to me into stubborn harshness. The ancient law of Athens gives me the right to demand she marry Demetrius or have her put to death.

Theseus What say you, Hermia? I know Demetrius is a worthy gentleman.

Hermia I wish for a moment my father could see with my eyes!

Theseus It is your duty to look through his eyes, fair maid.

Hermia I entreat your grace to pardon me. I ask that you tell me the worst thing that may befall me if I refuse to wed Demetrius.

Theseus Either to die the death or to live forever without a husband in a nunnery.

Hermia So will I grow, so live, so die, my lord.

Theseus Take some time to pause; and by the next new moon, the wedding day of my love and me, upon that day either prepare to die for disobedience to your father's will, wed Demetrius as he wishes, or agree to live as a nun for the rest of your life.

Demetrius Relent, sweet Hermia; and Lysander, yield thy crazed title to my certain right.

Lysander I am, my lord, as well possessed as he; my fortunes are just as great; and my love is more than his. Demetrius himself once loved Nedar's daughter, Helena, and won her soul. She now dotes upon this inconstant man.

Theseus I must confess that I have heard of this, and thought to speak of it with Demetrius; but I did not remember. But now, Demetrius and Egeus, both of you come with me, and I will counsel you privately. And you, fair Hermia, look to fit your fancies to your father's will.

Egeus With duty and desire we follow you.

Exit all but Lysander and Hermia.

Lysander How now, my love! Why is your cheek so pale? The course of true love never did run smooth. Hear me, Hermia. I have a widow aunt with great revenue, and she has no child. Her house is only seven leagues from Athens, and she respects me as her only son. There, gentle Hermia, may I marry thee, where Athenian law cannot pursue us. Steal forth from thy father's house tomorrow night, and meet me in the woods.

Hermia My good Lysander! I swear to thee, by Cupid's strongest bow, yes!

Lysander Keep promise, love. Look, here comes Helena.

Enter Helena.

Hermia Greetings, fair Helena!

Helena Call you me fair? If only I were as fair as thee. Demetrius loves your fairness. If only my ear should catch your voice, my eye your eye. O teach me how you look, and with what art you sway the motion of Demetrius' heart.

Hermia I frown upon him, yet he loves me still.

Helena O that your frowns would teach my smiles such a skill!

Hermia I give him curses, yet he gives me love. The more I hate, the more he follows me.

Helena The more I love, the more he hates me.

Hermia Take comfort, Helena. He no more shall see my face; Lysander and myself will leave this place.

Lysander Helena, we will tell you our secret. Tomorrow night, under full moon, Hermia and I will steal through Athens' gates.

Hermia We will meet in the woods and be gone from Athens forever. *(She turns to Lysander, taking his hands.)* Until tomorrow, Lysander.

Lysander Until then, my love.

Exit Lysander and Hermia.

Helena How happy others can be! Through Athens I am thought as fair as she. But what of that? Demetrius thinks not so. Love can transpose form and dignity. Love looks not with the eyes, but with the mind. But wait! I will tell Demetrius of

Hermia's plans, then to the woods he will go tomorrow night after her. If he only thanks me, that is the price I must pay; but I mean to have his love when he returns.

SCENE TWO *Quince's house in the city of Athens.*

Enter Quince, Snug, Bottom, Flute, Snout, and Starveling.

Quince Is all our company here?

Bottom Call everyone's name, man by man, according to the script.

Quince I have searched for the finest masters of acting in Athens. Here is the scroll of every man's name in our play to be performed before the duke and duchess on their wedding day.

Bottom First, good Peter Quince, tell us what the play is about, then read the names of the actors.

Quince Our play is called *The Most Lamentable Comedy, and Most Cruel Death of Pyramus and Thisby.*

Bottom A very good piece of work, I assure you, and very funny. Now, good Peter Quince, call forth your actors by the scroll.

Quince Answer as I call you.—Nick Bottom, the weaver.

Bottom Ready. Name what part I am for, and proceed.

Quince You, Nick Bottom, will play Pyramus.

Bottom Who is Pyramus?

Quince A lover who kills himself most gallantly for love.—Francis Flute, the bellows-mender.

Flute Here, Peter Quince.

Quince Flute, you must be Thisby.

Flute Who is Thisby? A wandering knight?

Quince It is the lady who Pyramus loves.

Flute O, no. Let me not play a woman; I have a beard coming.

Quince It matters not; you shall play it in a mask, and you may speak as small as you can in a woman's voice.

Bottom Proceed, Peter Quince.

Quince Robin Starveling, the tailor.

Starveling Here, Peter Quince.

Quince Robin Starveling, you must play Thisby's mother.—Tom Snout, the tinker.

Snout Here, Peter Quince.

Quince You will play Pyramus' father; and I, Thisby's father. Snug, the joiner, you play the lion. And that, I hope, is the making of a play.

Snug Have you written the lion's part yet? If you have, please let me have a copy, for I am slow of study and need plenty of time to memorize.

Quince You may do it without a written script, for it is nothing but roaring.

Bottom Let me play the lion, too. I will roar, and do every man's heart good to hear me. I shall roar, and I will make the duke say, "Let him roar again, let him roar again!"

Quince And you will do it too terribly, and frighten the duchess and ladies that they would shriek; and that would be enough to hang us all.

All That would hang us, every mother's son.

Quince Bottom, you can play no part but Pyramus; for Pyramus is a sweet-faced man, a proper man, a most gentleman-like man; therefore, you must play Pyramus.

Bottom Well, I will undertake it. What color beard would I best play it in?

Quince Whatever you wish.

Bottom I will color it in either straw color, orange tawny, purple-in-grain, or perfect yellow.

Quince Very well. Masters, here are your parts. *(He hands them each a script.)* I request that you memorize them by tomorrow night, and meet me in the palace wood where we can rehearse by moonlight. If we meet in the city, we will have many onlookers and our play will be known to all. I ask you, fail me not.

Bottom We will meet, and there we may rehearse most courageously. Take pains; be perfect. Adieu.

Quince At the duke's oak we meet.

❧ ACT TWO ❧

SCENE ONE The wood near Athens.

Enter, from opposite sides, a fairy and Puck.

Puck How now, fairy! From where do you wander?

Fairy Over hill, over dale, over park, over pale, through flood, through fire, I do wander everywhere. I serve the fairy queen. But farewell, thou lob of spirits. I'll now be gone; our queen and all her elves come here anon.

Puck The fairy king Oberon will come here for a celebration tonight; take care the queen comes not within his sight. Oberon is angry at the queen. She has with her a child stolen from an Indian king. She never had so sweet a changeling, and jealous Oberon wants the child for his servant. But the queen will not give him to Oberon. She loves him like her own child.

Fairy Are you not that knavish sprite named Robin Goodfellow, the one who frightens young maidens in the village? the one who misleads people traveling at night, laughing at their harm? Those that know you call you Puck.

Puck Thou speak'st right; I am that merry wanderer of the night. I jest with Oberon and make him smile with the pranks I play on others. Sometimes an old woman mistakes me for a stool, and I slip from under her and down she topples. Other times I lurk in a gossip's soup bowl, looking like a roasted crab, and when she drinks, against her lips I pinch! A merrier hour was never wasted there. But beware, fairy! Here comes Oberon.

Fairy And here comes my mistress, the queen! I wish that he were gone!

....

SCENE TWO *Enter Oberon with his servants from one side, and Titania with her servants from the other.*

....

Oberon Ill met by moonlight, proud Titania.

Titania What, jealous Oberon! Do you still want the child?

Oberon Am I not thy king?

Titania Then I must be thy lady; but I do not live as such.

Oberon Why should Titania cross her Oberon? I do but beg a little changeling boy to be my henchman.

Titania Set your heart at rest; the fairy land buys not the child from me. His mother was my friend, but being mortal, of that boy she did die; and for her sake I do rear up her boy. I will not part with him.

Oberon How long do you intend to stay in these woods?

Titania Perchance, till after Theseus' wedding day. If you wish, dance patiently in our round, and you may go with us. If not, shun me, and I will avoid thee as well.

Oberon Give me that boy, and I will go with thee.

Titania Not for thy fairy kingdom. Fairies, away!

Exit Titania, with her train.

Oberon Well, go thy way. Thou shall not leave these woods till I torment thee for this injury. Puck, come hither. *(Puck moves close to Oberon.)* Does thou remember once at the sea, I heard a mermaid on a dolphin's back making such sweet sounds with her voice that the rude sea grew calm at her song?

Puck I remember.

Oberon On that night, Cupid shot an arrow and missed. I know where it landed—on a little purple flower. The maidens call it Love-in-idleness. Fetch me that flower, Puck. The juice of that flower on sleeping eyelids will make any man or woman fall madly in love with the next live creature it sees.

Puck I'll have it for you in forty minutes.

Exit Puck.

Oberon Having this juice from the purple flower, I'll watch Titania when she is asleep, and drop the liquid in her eyes. The first thing she looks upon when she wakes, be it lion, bear, wolf, or bull, or meddling monkey, or busy ape—she shall pursue it with the soul of love. And when I break the spell, I will make her give the child to me. But who comes here? I shall be invisible and overhear their conference.

Enter Demetrius, and Helena, following him.

Demetrius I do not love you, so follow me not.

Helena You draw me here, I cannot help it. My heart is as true as steel.

Demetrius Do I entice you? Do I say nice things to you? Do I pretend to love you? Or do I speak the truth and tell you that I cannot love you?

Helena And for that I love you all the more.

Demetrius I shall run from thee and hide in the darkness, and leave you to the mercy of the wild beasts.

Helena Run when you will; I will follow.

Demetrius Let me go. Or, if you follow me, do not believe but I shall do thee mischief here in the wood.

Helena I'll follow thee and make a heaven of the underworld, to die upon the hand I love so well.

Exit Demetrius, with Helena following.

Oberon Fare thee well, nymph. Though he leaves this grove, thou shall find him and he shall seek thy love.

Re-enter Puck, holding the purple flower.

Oberon Welcome, wanderer. Hast thou the flower?

Puck Ay, here it is.

Oberon Good, give it to me. Now listen carefully. There is a bank where wild thyme grows; there Titania sleeps during the night. I'll streak her eyes with the juice of this flower

and make her full of fantasies. Take thou some of it, and look through this grove. A sweet Athenian lady is in love with a disdainful youth. Anoint his eyes with the flower juice, but only when you are certain that the lady is the next thing he sees. You will know the man by the Athenian clothing he wears. Take care, and meet me here at dawn.

Puck Fear not, my lord, your servant shall do so.

SCENE THREE *Another part of the wood.*

Enter Titania, with her train of servants.

Titania Come now fairies, sing me asleep; then to your offices, and let me rest.

The fairies hum a lullaby until Titania falls asleep. Exit fairies. Enter Oberon, who squeezes the flower juice on the sleeping Titania's eyelids.

Oberon What you see when you wake, it shall be thy true love. Be it cat, or bear, or boar with bristled hair, when you wake, it is thy dear. Wake when something vile is near.

Exit Oberon. Enter Lysander and Hermia.

Lysander Fair love, you are tired from this long walk. And truth be told, I have lost our way. Let us rest here.

Hermia I shall sleep upon this bank of flowers.

Lysander And I, under this tree. Good-night!

Hermia Until tomorrow.

They lie down and fall sleep. Enter Puck.

Puck Through the forest I have gone. But wait! Who is this? Clothing of Athens doth he wear. This is he, my master said, who despised the Athenian maid who sleeps nearby. Upon thy eyes I throw all the power this charm doth owe. When you wake, let love set his seat on thy eyelid. So awake when I am gone, for I must return to Oberon.

Puck places the flower juice on Lysander's eyelids, and exits. Enter Demetrius and Helena, running.

Helena Stay, even if thou kill me, sweet Demetrius.

Demetrius I charge thee, do not haunt me thus.

Helena O, will thou leave me? Do not so.

Demetrius Stay, on thy peril; I alone will go.

Exit Demetrius.

Helena O, I am out of breath in this fond chase! But who is here? Lysander?

Lysander *(awakening and seeing Helena)* And run through fire I will for thy sweet sake! Helena, it is you! You are the one I have always loved. Where is Demetrius? That vile name will perish on my sword!

Helena Do not say so, Lysander; say not so. Though he loves your Hermia, she loves only you. Be content.

Lysander Content with Hermia? It is not Hermia but Helena I love. Who will not change a chicken for a dove?

Helena Why do you tease me so? When did I deserve this scorn? Is it not enough that I never can deserve a sweet look from Demetrius' eye, but you must flout my insufficiency? Farewell, Lysander. I must confess I thought you a more gentle man.

Exit Helena.

Lysander She sees not Hermia. Hermia, sleep thou there and never come near me again!

Exit Lysander.

Hermia *(awakening)* Help me, Lysander, help me! Do thy best to pluck this crawling serpent from my chest! O, me! It was just a dream. Methought a serpent ate my heart away, and you were smiling at his cruel prey. Lysander, where are you? I swoon almost with fear. I must find you!

Exit Hermia.

 ACT THREE

SCENE ONE *The same wood. Titania is lying asleep.*

Enter Quince, Snug, Bottom, Flute, Snout, and Starveling.

Bottom Are we all here?

Quince Here's a marvelous convenient place for our rehearsal! This green plot shall be our stage, and we will do it in action as if before the duke.

Bottom Peter Quince?

Quince What say you, bully Bottom?

Bottom There are things in this comedy of Pyramus and Thisby that will never please. First, Pyramus must draw a sword to kill himself, which the ladies in the audience will not like. How do you answer that?

Starveling I believe we must leave the killing out, when all is done.

Bottom Not necessary; I know how to fix this. Write me a prologue saying that we will do no harm with our swords, and that Pyramus is not really killed. And tell them that I, Pyramus, am not Pyramus, but Bottom the weaver. This will put them out of fear.

Quince Well, we will have such a prologue, and it shall be written.

Snout Will not the ladies be afraid of the lion?

Starveling I fear it, I promise you.

Bottom Masters, you ought to consider that bringing a lion among ladies is a most dreadful thing; for there is none more fearful animal than a living lion, and we ought to look to it.

Snout Therefore, another prologue must tell that he is not a lion.

Bottom You must say his name, and half his face must be seen through the lion's neck; and he himself must speak through the mask, saying, "Fair ladies, I request you not tremble or fear. I am not really a lion, but a man as other men are."

Quince Well it shall be so.

Snug Does the moon shine the night we do our play?

Quince Yes. We must have someone come in with a lantern and say he comes to represent moonshine.

Bottom And some man or other must represent a wall. Let him hold his fingers thus, and through that cranny shall Pyramus and Thisby whisper.

Quince Very well. Come, sit down, every mother's son, and rehearse your parts. Pyramus, you begin. When you have spoken your speech, enter into that hedge, and so everyone according to his cue.

Enter Puck, who hides behind a tree.

Puck What home-spuns have we swaggering here, so near the cradle of the fairy queen? What, a play! I'll be an auditor; and an actor too, perhaps, if I see cause!

Quince Speak, Pyramus. Thisby, stand forth.

Pyramus "Thisby, the flowers of odious savours sweet . . . "

Quince Odors, odors—not odious!

Pyramus " . . . odors savours sweet.
So hath thy breath, my dearest Thisby.
But hark! A voice!"

Exit Bottom into the hedge.

Puck A stranger Pyramus than ever played here!

Exit Puck, following Bottom.

Flute Must I speak now?

Quince Aye, you must; for you must understand he goes to see a noise he heard, and will come again.

Thisby "Most radiant Pyramus, most lily-white of hue; I'll meet thee, Pyramus, at Ninny's tomb."

Quince Ninus' tomb, not Ninny's tomb! And you say that part after you answer to Pyramus. Wait for your cue!

Re-enter Puck, and Bottom with a donkey's head in place of his own.

Pyramus "If I were fair, Thisby, I were only yours."

Quince O monstrous! O strange! We are haunted! Run, everyone! Help!

Exit Quince; Snug; Flute; Snout; Starveling; and Puck, who is laughing.

Bottom Why do they run away? This is knavery of them to scare me so.

Re-enter Snout.

Snout O Bottom, thou art changed! What is that on your shoulders?

Bottom What do you see?

Exit Snout. Re-enter Quince.

Quince Bless thee, Bottom! Thou art translated!

Exit Quince.

Bottom I see their knavery. This is to make an ass of me, to frighten me. They shall hear that I am not afraid. *(He sings.)* "The ousel rooster so black of hue, with orange-tawny bill; the throstle with his note so true, the wren with little quill . . ."

Titania *(awakening)* What angel wakes me from my flowery bed? Gentle mortal, sing again. Mine ear is much enamored of thy note. On first view, to swear, I love thee!

Bottom I do not deserve your love. I only wish to escape from this wood.

Titania Do not desire to go out of this wood. Thou shall remain here, as I do love thee. Therefore, go with me; I'll give thee fairies to attend to thee. Peaseblossom! Cobweb! Moth! Mustardseed!

Enter Peaseblossom, Cobweb, Moth, and Mustardseed.

Peaseblossom Ready.

Cobweb And I.

Moth And I.

Mustardseed And I.

All Fairies Where shall we go?

Titania Be kind and courteous to this gentleman. Feed him with honey, apricots, and dewberries. Nod to him, elves, and do him courtesies.

All Fairies Hail, mortal!

Bottom I am pleased to meet you all.

Titania Come, wait upon him, and lead him to my bower.

SCENE TWO *Another part of the wood.*

Enter Oberon.

Oberon I wonder if Titania is awake, and what it was that first came to her eye.

Enter Puck.

Oberon Here comes my messenger. How now, mad spirit?

Puck The queen is in love with a monster. I affixed an ass's head to an actor in the forest, and she, upon awakening, saw him first.

Oberon This has turned out better than I had hoped! Hast thou also fixed the eyes of the young Athenian that I bid thee do?

Puck Yes, while he was sleeping near the Athenian woman.

Enter Hermia and Demetrius.

Oberon Stand close; this is the same Athenian we speak of.

Puck This is the woman, but not the man.

Hermia Where is my Lysander? What have you done to him? Ah, good Demetrius, will thou give him to me?

Demetrius I would rather give his carcass to my hounds.

Hermia Hast thou slain him then? Hast thou killed him sleeping? O, henceforth be never numbered among men!

Demetrius You are wasting your breath; I am not guilty of Lysander's blood.

Hermia Tell me then that he is well.

Demetrius And if I could, what will I get?

Hermia The privilege to see me no more. See me no more, whether he be dead or not!

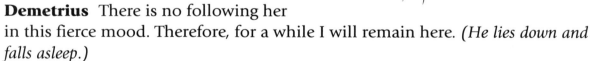

Exit Hermia.

Demetrius There is no following her in this fierce mood. Therefore, for a while I will remain here. *(He lies down and falls asleep.)*

Oberon What have you done? You have mistakenly placed the love juice on the wrong man! Go and find Helena of Athens; she is likely sick and pale. I'll charm this man's eyes when she appears.

Puck I go, I go; look, how I go.

Exit Puck.

Oberon Flower of this purple die, hit with Cupid's archery, sink in the apple of his eye. When his love he doth espy, let her shine as gloriously as the Venus of the sky.

Re-enter Puck.

Puck Sir, Helena is here at hand; and the youth, pleading for her love.

Oberon Stand aside. The noise they make will cause Demetrius to wake.

Enter Lysander and Helena.

Lysander Why should you think I woo in jest? I speak the truth; I love you.

Helena Those vows are Hermia's; will you give them to her?

Lysander I had no judgment when to her I swore. Demetrius loves her, and not you.

Demetrius *(awakening and seeing Helena)* O Helena, goddess, you are perfect, divine! To what, my love, shall I compare thine eyes? O, let me kiss thy hand!

Helena O spite! I see you are all bent to set against me for your merriment. If you were civil and knew courtesy, you would not do me this much injury.

Lysander You are unkind, Demetrius; be not so. You love Hermia, this you know I know.

Demetrius Lysander, keep thy Hermia; I will not. If ever I loved her, all that love is gone. My heart is now with Helena, and there it will remain.

Re-enter Hermia.

Hermia Lysander, why did thou leave me so?

Lysander Why should I stay, when love told me to go?

Hermia What love stole you from my side?

Lysander My love for fair Helena. The hate I bear you made me leave you so.

Hermia You speak not as you think. It cannot be!

Helena Lo, she is one of this confederacy! Injurious Hermia! Most ungrateful maid! Have you conspired with these two men to bait me with this foul derision?

Hermia I am amazed at your passionate words. I scorn you not. It seems that *you* scorn *me*. You thief of love! Have you come by night and stolen my love's heart from him?

Helena Fie, fie! Will you tear impatient answers from my tongue? You counterfeit, you puppet!

Hermia Puppet? Why so? How did you prevail? Because I am shorter than you, thou painted maypole? I am not so low that my nails would fail to reach your eyes!

Helena I will take my leave of you, my former friend. To Athens I will return.

Hermia Get you gone, then. Who keeps you here?

Helena A foolish heart that I leave here behind.

Hermia What? With Lysander?

Helena With Demetrius.

Lysander *(to Hermia)* Get you gone, dwarf; you minimus, of knot-grass made. You bead, you acorn.

Demetrius Let her alone, Lysander. Let the two of us depart together. We can settle this matter quickly.

Exit Lysander and Demetrius.

Hermia You, mistress, all this trouble is because of you! Go not back.

Helena I will not trust you here alone, nor can I stay in your company. Farewell.

Exit Helena.

Hermia I am amazed, and know not what to say.

Exit Hermia.

Oberon *(to Puck)* This is your fault. Did you make a mistake, or did you do this on purpose?

Puck Believe me, king of shadows, I made a mistake. Did you not tell me I would know the man by the Athenian garment he had on?

Oberon Thou now see'st two men seeking a place to fight. Therefore, Robin, overcast the night with drooping black fog to lead them astray from one another. Then, tired with wandering, they will sleep. Crush this flower juice into Lysander's eye, to take from him all error with his might. When they next awake, this derision shall seem a dream.

Puck I shall. Here comes one.

Re-enter Lysander.

Lysander Where art thou, proud Demetrius? Speak now.

Puck *(imitating Demetrius)* Here, villain; drawn and ready. Where art thou?

Lysander I will be with thee straight.

Puck Follow me then, to plainer ground.

Exit Lysander, following the voice. Re-enter Demetrius.

Demetrius Lysander! Where are you? Thou runaway, thou coward, art thou fled?

Puck *(imitating Lysander)* Thou coward! Art thou bragging to the stars? Come, little child, I'll whip thee with a stick. I need draw no sword on thee.

Exit Demetrius. Re-enter Lysander.

Lysander He goes before me and still dares me on. When I come where he calls, then he is gone. I am tired, and will rest here for awhile. *(He lies down and falls asleep.)*

Puck *(as Lysander)* Ho, ho! Coward, why comest thou not?

Re-enter Demetrius.

Demetrius Where art thou now? Thou dare not stand, nor look me in the face.

Puck *(as Lysander)* Come hither! I am here.

Demetrius Thou mock'st me. Thou shall pay dearly if ever I see thy face by daylight. Now, go thy way. Faintness keeps me from following thee. *(He lies down and falls asleep.)*

Re-enter Helena.

Helena O weary night! O long and tedious night, abate thy hours! Upon daylight, I will find my way back to Athens, away from these whose company I detest. And sleep, steal me away from my own company. *(She lies down and falls asleep.)*

Puck Yet but three? Just one more I need, to finish my deed.

Re-enter Hermia.

Hermia Never so weary, never so in woe, I can no further crawl, no further go. Here I will rest till the break of day. Heavens shield Lysander if they mean a fray! *(She lies down and falls asleep.)*

Puck On the ground, sleep sound. I'll apply to your eye, gentle lover, a remedy. *(He squeezes the flower juice on Lysander's eyes.)* When thou wake'st, thou will take true delight in the sight of thy former lady's eye. And all shall be well.

Exit Puck.

❧ ACT FOUR ❧

SCENE ONE   *The same. Lysander, Demetrius, Helena, and Hermia are lying asleep.*

Enter Titania and Bottom; Peaseblossom, Cobweb, Moth, Mustardseed, and other fairies; and Oberon behind, unseen.

Titania   Come, sit thee down on this flowery bed, while I kiss thy fair large ears.

Bottom   Where's Peaseblossom?

Peaseblossom   Ready.

Bottom   Scratch my head, Peaseblossom.

Titania   Will you hear some music, my sweet love?

Bottom   Let's have the tongs and the bones.

Titania   Or, sweet love, say what you desire to eat.

Bottom   I could munch some good dry oats. But first, sleep comes upon me. *(He falls asleep.)*

Titania   Sleep, thou, and I will wind thee in my arms. Fairies, be gone.

Exit fairies.

Titania   O, how I love thee! How I dote on thee! *(She falls asleep next to Bottom.)*

Enter Puck.

Oberon *(advancing)* Welcome, good Robin. Do you see this sweet sight? But now her dotage I begin to pity. She has fallen so deeply in love with this creature that she agreed to give me the child I sought. Now I can remove the spell, and you must remove the head from this Athenian. Now, my Titania, wake you, my sweet queen.

Titania My Oberon! What visions I have seen! Methought I was in love with an ass.

Oberon There lies your love, next to you.

Titania How came these things to pass? O, how mine eyes loathe his visage now!

Oberon Silence awhile. Robin, take off his head.

Puck Now, Athenian, when thou wakest, with thine own fool's eyes peep.

Oberon Then, my queen, in silence sad, trip we after the night's shade.

Titania Come, my lord; and in our flight, tell me how it came this night, that I was sleeping here was found with these mortals on the ground.

Horns sound in the distance.

Exit Puck, Oberon, and Titania. Enter Theseus, Hippolyta, Egeus, and attendants.

Theseus Where is the forester? We shall hunt for a large boar for our feast. *(He notices the four sleeping Athenians.)* But soft! What nymphs are these?

Egeus My lord, this is my daughter Hermia, here asleep; and this, Lysander; this Demetrius is; this, Helena. I wonder how they got here together.

Theseus Speak, Egeus; is this not the day that Hermia should give answer of her choice?

Egeus It is, my lord.

Lysander, Demetrius, Helena, and Hermia wake up, startled.

Lysander Pardon, my lord.

Theseus All of you, please rise. How came you here together? I know you two are rival enemies.

Lysander My lord, I shall reply amazedly, still half asleep, but I cannot truly say how I came here. But I think I came with Hermia to escape the peril of Athenian law.

Egeus Enough, enough! My lord, you have enough; I beg the law upon his head. My daughter is to be Demetrius' wife.

Demetrius My lord, fair Helena told me of their plans, and I followed them into the woods. I cannot say by what power, my lord, but my love to Hermia seems to be melted as the snow. My heart belongs to Helena.

Theseus Fair lovers, what fortunate circumstance! Of this discourse we will hear more. Egeus, I will overbear your will. For in the temple by and by with us, these couples shall be married. Away with us to Athens, and we'll hold a feast. Come, Hippolyta.

Exit Theseus, Hippolyta, Egeus, the four young Athenians, and attendants.

Bottom *(awakening, confused)* When my cue comes, call me, and I will answer. My next line is, "Most fair Pyramus." Heigh, ho! Peter Quince! Flute! Snout! They left, and I fell asleep. I have had a most rare vision. I have had a dream, past the wit of man to say what dream it was. Man is but an ass if he go about to expound on his dream. I will get Peter Quince to write a ballad of this dream. It shall be called Bottom's Dream, because it has no bottom; and I will sing it at the end of the play.

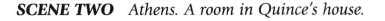

SCENE TWO *Athens. A room in Quince's house.*

Enter Quince, Flute, Snout, and Starveling.

Quince Have you searched at Bottom's house? Is he home yet?

Starveling He cannot be heard of.

Flute If he doesn't come, the play is marred!

Quince He is the best actor of any man in Athens; only he can play Pyramus.

Flute O sweet bully Bottom! Where has he gone?

Enter Bottom.

Quince Bottom! O most courageous day! O most happy hour! Tell us what happened!

Bottom Not a word of me. All I will tell you is the duke has dined. Get your costumes together, good strings to your beards, and meet presently at the palace. Every man look over his part; and most dear actors, eat no onions nor garlic, for we are to utter sweet breath, and they will say it is a sweet comedy. Away! Away!

❧ ACT FIVE ❧

SCENE ONE *Athens. The palace of Theseus.*

Enter Theseus, Hippolyta, Philostrate, Egeus, lords, and attendants.

Theseus Here come the lovers, full of joy and mirth. Call Philostrate.

Enter Lysander, Demetrius, Hermia, and Helena.

Philostrate Here, mighty Theseus.

Theseus What is planned for our entertainment this evening?

Philostrate There is a play, my lord. But it is not for you. It is nothing, unless you can find sport in their intents, extremely stretched to do you service.

Theseus I will hear that play; for never can anything be amiss, when simpleness and duty tender it. Go, bring them in; and take your places, ladies.

Exit Philostrate. Enter Bottom, Flute, Snug, Snout, and Starveling as Pyramus, Thisby, Lion, Wall, and Moonshine.

Pyramus "O, what a grim night! O wall; O sweet wall that stands between her father's ground and mine! Show me a crack through which I can look!"

Wall holds up his fingers.

Pyramus *(looking through Wall's fingers)* "Thanks, courteous wall. But what see I? No Thisby do I see. O wicked wall, through whom I see no bliss!"

Enter Thisby.

Thisby "O wall, often you have heard my cries, for parting my Pyramus and me!"

Pyramus "I see a voice. I will return to the crack to spy. Thisby! O Thisby, kiss me through the crack in the wall."

Thisby "I kiss the wall's crack, not your lips at all."

Pyramus "Will you meet me at Ninny's tomb, right away?"

Thisby "I come without delay."

Exit Pyramus and Thisby.

Wall I have done my part, and now be done, away Wall doth go.

Exit Wall.

Hippolyta This is the silliest stuff I ever heard.

Theseus If we imagine no worse of them than they of themselves, they may pass for excellent men. Here come two noble beasts, a moon and a lion.

Enter Lion and Moonshine.

Lion "Ladies, do not fear. Know that I am Snug the joiner, only a man."

Moonshine "I am the man in the moon; that is all I have to say."

Enter Thisby.

Thisby "This is old Ninny's tomb. Where is my love?"

Lion *(He stands a moment, confused.)* "Oh."

Lion roars and Thisby runs away.

Demetrius Well roared, Lion.

Theseus Well run, Thisby.

Hippolyta Well shone, Moon.

Exit Lion.

Demetrius And then came Pyramus.

Lysander And so the lion vanished.

Re-enter Pyramus.

Pyramus "What dreadful dole is here? How can it be? O dainty duck! O dear! Thy mantle, stained with blood! Since the lion has here devoured my dear, that lived, that loved, that looked with cheer. Out sword, and wound the heart of Pyramus! *(He stabs himself.)* Thus I die, thus, thus! Now I am dead! My soul is in the sky. Moon, take they flight! Now I die, die, die!" *(He dies.)*

Exit Moonshine.

Hippolyta How chance Moonshine is gone before Thisby comes back and finds her lover?

Theseus She will find him by starlight, and her passion ends the play.

Enter Thisby.

Hippolyta Methinks, she should not use a long one for such a Pyramus. I hope she will be brief.

Thisby "Asleep, my love? What, dead, my dove? O Pyramus, arise! Speak, speak! Dead? A tomb must cover thy sweet eyes. Come, trusty sword, my breast imbrue. *(She stabs herself.)* And farewell, friends; thus Thisby ends. Adieu, adieu, adieu." *(She dies.)*

Theseus Moonshine and Lion are left to bury the dead.

Demetrius Ay, and Wall too.

Bottom No, I assure you; the wall is down that parted their fathers. Will it please you to see the epilogue?

Theseus No epilogue, I pray you. Your play needs no excuse. Never excuse, for when the players are all dead, there need none to be blamed. Let your epilogue alone; it's now midnight. Sweet friends, to bed.

....
SCENE TWO *The same, after everyone has gone to bed.*
....

Enter Puck.

Puck Now it is the time of night, that the graves, all gaping wide, every one lets forth its sprite. And we fairies, that do run from the presence of the sun, following darkness like a dream. Not a mouse shall disturb this hallowed house.

Enter Oberon and Titania with their train.

Titania Hand in hand, with fairy grace, we will sing, and bless this place.

Oberon Now until the break of day, through this house each fairy stray. So shall all the couples three, ever true in loving be. Through this palace with sweet peace, ever shall in safety rest, and the owner of it blest. Trip away! Make no stay; meet me all by break of day.

Exit Oberon, Titania, and their train.

Puck If we shadows have offended, think but this, and all is mended; that you have but slumbered here, while these visions did appear. And this weak and idle theme, no more yielding but a dream. So, good-night unto you all. Give me your hands, if we be friends, and Robin shall restore amends.

ACT ONE

adieu good-bye

baubles showy trinkets

befall become of

bewitched under a spell

dotes shows excessive affection

fair beautiful

entreat ask; beg

inconstant changes frequently without reason

joiner one who makes objects that join wood pieces

lamentable sorrowful; sad

relent give in

revenue wealth

transpose change

vexation agitation; torment

well possessed knowledgeable

woo'd sought affection

ACT TWO

anoint apply; rub on

anon shortly

changeling infant secretly exchanged for another

charge order; command

conference conversation

despised hated

disdainful proud; scornful

entice tempt

flout speak sarcastically

fond eager from desire

henchman honored servant

hither here

jest joke

knavish full of trickery

lob country bumpkin

mortal human

nymph young, beautiful woman

offices duties of servants

perchance by chance

peril risk

perish die

scorn insult

shun avoid deliberately

sprite supernatural being

swoon faint

vile disgusting

ACT THREE

abate shorten

astray wandering

attend to look after

auditor one who listens (as in an audience)

bead very small thing

bent intense inclination

bid ask; command

bower lady's private dwelling

bully term of endearment

carcass dead body

civil good-mannered

confederacy conspiracy

conspired plotted

counterfeit deceitful

cranny small crack

derision scorn

detest hate

drawn sword out, ready to fight

enamored in love with

espy see

fie expression of disgust

foul abusive

fray fight

henceforth from now on

home-spuns clowns

hue color

knavery trickery

knot-grass common weed

maypole tall flowered pole in the center of May Day sports and games

minimus small creature

mocks makes fun of

odious disgusting; repulsive

ousel blackbird

painted fake

plainer flatter; more level

prevail persuade effectively

prologue introduction to a written work

puppet small figure

quill feather

remedy something that corrects a wrong

savours perfumes; scent

slain killed

spite outrage

straight right away

swaggering boasting

tedious long; laboring

throstle thrush (singing bird)

translated changed

woe grief; lament

ACT FOUR

ballad song

discourse conversation; talk

expound explain in detail

loathe hate

marred spoiled; ruined

overbear override

rare unusual

rival competing

tongs and bones simple, rustic musical instruments

utter exhale

visage appearance

wit intelligence; mental abilities

ACT FIVE

amends compensation; improvement

amiss faulty

bliss complete happiness

dole sorrowful object

epilogue final scene of a play summarizing the main action

hallowed greatly respected

idle foolish; silly

imbrue stain with blood

intents purpose; intentions

mantle cloak

mirth joy; happiness

offended insulted

slumbered slept

sport fun

tender regard favorably

"All the world's a stage, and all the men and women merely players." This quote from Shakespeare's delightful comedy *As You Like It* is a great way to begin your study of Shakespeare. Ask students what they think this quote means. Explain that "players" are actually "actors." Shakespeare meant that throughout our lives, we play many different roles—children, teenagers, and adults; daughters, sons, mothers, fathers, cousins, friends, workers, and so on. We also "act" within our life roles. Play-acting is a part of everyday existence. Ask students when they might "act" in real life. Invite them to act out an incident from their lives for the class (for example, a problem with a sibling, a funny incident with a family member or friend, or an embarrassing moment). Students can have lots of fun with this; encourage them to be creative, yet true to life.

 Ask students if they have ever seen a stage play. Discuss the difference between acting onstage, in the movies, or on TV. In Shakespeare's time, there were no TVs, movies, radios, or video games, so entertainment usually came in the form of drama. Drama did not begin with Shakespeare. Plays were watched with rapt attention by theatregoers many centuries before him. Drama is thought to have developed from many sources—an outgrowth of religious ceremonies to appease the gods; songs at grave sites or about heroes, extolling their virtues; to preach morals to the masses; and simply to satisfy people's natural love for storytelling and entertainment. Drama was and still is a way to "get away from it all" and have a good time. It creates an opportunity for us to laugh at ourselves as we see life reflected in the many human characters and situations portrayed before us.

Showing videotapes of Shakespearean plays helps children understand the nuances of drama, and how Shakespeare's language and characterization bring his stories to life. Many of Shakespeare's plays are available on videotape. Watch a video and/or compare one video interpretation to another. Make sure to view videos before showing them to your class, as some material may be unsuitable due to language or adult situations. However, don't let videos replace the reading and performing of plays by your students. Shakespeare is meant to be experienced as a live performance.

SHAKESPEAREAN COMEDY

"The tragic tale of Romeo and Juliet *becomes a comedy in* A Midsummer Night's Dream. *Appreciation depends upon entering the comic world and accepting its artifice, no matter how improbable."*

—Norrie Epstein

 One of the many joys of Shakespearean comedy is Shakespeare's flair for sarcasm and his use of witty, barbed, yet comic insults. His characters insult everything from hypocrisy to personal hygiene. In *A Midsummer Night's Dream*, Act III, Scene II, Helena and Hermia exchange stinging insults such as *painted maypole, counterfeit*, and *puppet*. Lysander even joins in with *minimus, of knot-grass made; bead;* and *acorn*. The absurdity of the scene adds to the humor of these offensive remarks. Other favorite Shakespearean barbs include *scullion, rampallion, fustilarian*, and *baggage*. Most of these terms were popular during Shakespeare's time, and his audience loved to witness Shakespeare's skill at stringing insults together into long, rapturous invectives.

Shakespearean comedies are much like tragedies with happy endings. In comedies, the same tragic circumstances and obstacles are introduced, but the characters avoid tragedy by using their wit, disguising themselves as other people, receiving intervention from "the gods," or any one of a myriad of improbable, yet successful events. Often these events are out of a character's control, such as when well-laid plans go awry or when he or she is confounded by mistaken identities. For example, in *A Midsummer Night's Dream*, characters enter the "enchanted wood," (the term *wood* meant *mad* in Elizabethan English) in which they transcend reality. Fairies divert the unknowing "mortals'" original paths, at first creating hilarious confusion, and finally restoring harmony. Hermia's and Lysander's probable deaths are diverted, Helena gets the man she loves, Oberon and Titania make peace with each other, and three happy couples get married.

While in tragedies characters are confronted with their own mortality and must take responsibility for their choices and actions, comedies steer characters away from their "tragic ends" by providing opportunities for second chances. There's always another chance for a character to redeem him- or herself. The improbable becomes probable; the unbelievable, believable; and the fantastical, reasonable. It is these qualities that make Shakespearean comedies such a delightful diversion from "real life." We know that the "cycle" will be complete, the beginning will become the end, and all sanity and joy restored.

ELEMENTS OF A STORY

Before reading the summary of the play to your students, familiarize them with the elements of a story. Write the following terms on the board and discuss what they mean with students. Tell them to look for these story elements and consider the following questions as they listen to the play's summary.

Protagonist—hero

Antagonist—villain

Sequence—the order in which events occur

Suspense—the tension and excitement created by not knowing a story's outcome

Plot—what the story is about

Climax—the scene or event with the highest dramatic tension (suspense) that creates the most drama or brings about a turning point in the action

Dialogue—words spoken by the characters

Mood—comedic, tragic, dramatic, and so on. The plot and characters determine the mood of the play (in this instance, comedic).

Ask students:

- Who do you think is the protagonist? the antagonist? Does a story need both a protagonist and antagonist? Why? *(to provide conflict, interest, contrast)*

- Did events in the story happen sequentially? Was there an easily-identifiable beginning, middle, and end? Why is sequence important in a story? *(so readers won't be confused; so the story makes sense)*

- Did the plot keep you interested? Did it portray a "fairy tale" or "comic" theme?

- Was the story suspenseful? Were you anxious about what was going to happen? What part or parts of the story were most suspenseful?

- What scene or scenes were the climax of the story? What event or events sealed the fate of the protagonist(s)?

- Did the language and dialogue seem authentic and true to life?

- Did the comedic mood persist throughout the play? Were moments of tension quickly relieved by this mood?

THE LANGUAGE OF SHAKESPEARE

At first, "Shakespearean language" can seem overwhelming to students. Many students have heard Shakespeare quoted, but have no idea what these quotes mean. Though the language may seem complex, it was common in England at the time the plays were written. It's no wonder students may feel overwhelmed reading even an edited version of a Shakespearean play. It's been estimated that he uses between 25,000 and 29,000 different words in his plays and poems! But among all the "thees" and "thous" are many common, everyday expressions students will be amazed to know originated with Shakespeare (or "the bard"). Write several of the following Shakespearean expressions on the board and invite students to guess what they mean. They'll be surprised at how these expressions have endured through time.

Apple of her eye

Bated breath

Budge an inch

Dead as a door nail

Eating me out of house and home

Eyesore

For goodness' sake

The game is up

Good riddance

Green-eyed monster

Household words

Knock, knock, who's there?

Laughingstock

The naked truth

Neither rhyme nor reason

One fell swoop

The primrose path

Such stuff as dreams are made on

Suit the action to the word

Sweets to the sweet

To thine own self be true

Too much of a good thing

Tower of strength

Wear my heart on my sleeve

What's done is done

If you decide to produce the play, you can make it as small or as large a production as you like. You may decide on just an "in-class" production, maybe inviting one or two classes to the performance; or you may want to perform for parents or the whole school. Decide which experience would most benefit your students and meet your classroom needs. When deciding the kind of production you want, consider the time you will need to invest and your classroom budget. It's advantageous for students to be able to perform more than once so they can evaluate and discuss areas for improvement.

 Discuss with students which type of production they prefer. Do they want a "classic" Shakespearean production, or do they want to get creative with their interpretation? Students can modernize the play, set it in a different time and/or place, or they can interject their own vernacular. There are many innovative ways to approach a Shakespearean production, so encourage students to brainstorm how they can make theirs original and interesting. Remind them that the fun of putting on a play is in the *process*, not necessarily the *performance*. Make it simple (props, costumes, scenery) so students will get the most out of the experience.

When deciding the kind of production you want, consider the time you will need to invest and your classroom budget.

 Most students will want to act in the play, and there's a good chance that several will want the leading roles. Since one purpose of performing plays is to increase self-esteem and self-confidence, it wouldn't make sense to choose only the most poised, confident students in the class. On the other hand, choosing a cast of shy, introverted actors will lessen the strength of and interest in the play. If possible, try and balance your cast. It's also helpful to choose actors who will help each other develop their parts in the friendly spirit of cooperation. Since there are fewer female than male roles, allow girls to play boys' parts and vice versa. Consider the following questions when choosing actors.

- **Does the student have a voice that carries? If not, can he or she bring up the voice level?**

- **Does the student show imagination and enthusiasm for the part?**

- **Does he or she have "stage presence"?**

- **Can the student think on his or her feet and bring the role to life?**

Auditions can be intimidating and possibly embarrassing for many students. Instead of having them audition for the entire class, invite small student groups to audition different roles for the play. During tryouts, encourage groups to offer encouragement and constructive criticism. "Can you look more at the audience?" is obviously better than "He never looks at the audience. He's terrible!" Before tryouts begin, discuss with students how to give constructive criticism in a kind, helpful, and respectful way. Write a list of rules on the board (e.g., *Be positive; Critique the "work," not the person*; and so on). As an alternative, invite students to write comments on note cards and give them to you. Read only those comments that are truly "constructive" and helpful to the performing student. Remind students that there is no one "right" way to do Shakespeare. A diversity of characterizations only adds dimension to the production. Invite groups to brainstorm each role and discuss their ideas with auditioning students.

 Even if your class is large, you can still get everyone involved in the production. Many students will want to act in the play, but some may prefer to work "behind the scenes." Emphasize that *all* jobs are important to a production. Invite interested students to "apply" for the following jobs by writing a short paragraph about why they would be good at a particular task, or you can simply hold "interviews" with individual students. Encourage them to have first and second choices, so everyone has a chance to do something he or she enjoys.

DIRECTOR

You may want to assume this responsibility, using one or two student assistants. The director helps place actors and scenery in the correct places, reminds actors when and how to project their voices, and keeps rehearsals structured. This is a difficult task, so make sure you choose students who aren't too "bossy." Many a production has crumbled because everyone resented the director's bossy ways.

UNDERSTUDIES

Necessary only for the leading roles. If there is more than one performance, they may play the leads the second time.

PROMPTER

Stands offstage during rehearsals and performances, and whispers lines and/or hints for the actors in case they forget their lines or where they should be onstage.

STAGE MANAGER AND ASSISTANT

Ensure that production is going smoothly and all scenery and props are in place.

MAKEUP ARTISTS

Decide on and apply makeup to actors before performances. You may want to have two or three students for this job. Call local cosmetology schools or colleges with theater departments for help.

Critique the "work," not the person.

COSTUMERS

Research the time period in which the play takes place, and create costumes from available materials. (Ask parents to donate old clothes and fabric scraps.) Simple costumes such as tunics can be made from large shirts cinched with belts, and sweatpants can be pulled up to look like Renaissance-period pants.

LIGHTING SPECIALIST

Works with the director to manipulate lighting for dramatic effects.

CURTAIN SPECIALIST

Raises and lowers the curtain at the appropriate times.

SCENERY AND PROP CREW

Finds and/or makes appropriate scenery and props for the play, sets up and takes down scenery during performances, cleans the stage and "theater" after performances.

ADVERTISING AND PUBLICITY CREW

Makes posters advertising the play. If you're inviting the whole school, write ads about the play and have them announced over the school intercom. If your production is going to be large, you might consider advertising it in your local newspaper or on your local public-access channel.

PLAYBILL WRITERS AND ILLUSTRATORS

Design and write a simple playbill with short blurbs about Shakespeare, the play, actors, scenes, and so on. This will add a nice dimension to your production.

TICKET TAKER

Necessary if you have parents coming to the performances. Most school plays are free, but you can "sell" tickets in exchange for a can of food for a local homeless shelter, a can of pet food or supplies for a local animal shelter, or other charitable donations.

USHERS

Show people to their seats and make certain "unruly" students keep quiet during performances.

VIDEOGRAPHER

Videotapes performances. This is great not only for critiquing the play later, but also authenticates the experience for students. They will love watching themselves on television. You may even want to make copies for families and friends to keep!

A Midsummer Night's Dream

performed by
Room 12

Unrequited love, forbidden love, and love confused between mortals and fairies—all cured by a magic flower!

To inspire students to think critically and form opinions, offer several of the following journal ideas for discussion, reflection, and writing.

⌘ ACT ONE ⌘

▓ According to Lysander, "The course of true love never did run smooth." Agree or disagree with this quote by providing supporting evidence from the play, real life, TV shows, and/or movies.

▓ Helena tells her best friend's secret to Demetrius—that Hermia and Lysander are eloping. Was it wrong of her to do this? Write about a time you told a secret. How did you feel? Did the person whose secret you told find out? What were the consequences of this act?

▓ Hermia and Lysander believe they have no choice except to run away together so they can get married. Discuss the pros and cons of running away from a problem. What would you do in Hermia's and Lysander's situation? Do you think they're making the right choice? What are some other options they could consider, if any?

▓ Hermia takes control over her life when she refuses to marry Demetrius and runs away with Lysander. Helena, on the other hand, follows Demetrius, hoping he will return her affections after hearing of the elopement. Discuss these two women according to their decisions. Is it better to make your own fate or trust that things will eventually turn out the way you want them? What do Hermia's and Helena's actions reveal about their personalities?

▓ Hermia takes a big risk by running away with Lysander. Under Athenian law, she could be put to death by disobeying her father! Write a letter from either Hermia or Lysander to Egeus, Hermia's father, trying to convince him to let Hermia and Lysander marry. In the play, Demetrius had formerly "wooed" Helena, and then deserted her. Can this information be used as a way to make Egeus realize that perhaps Lysander is a better match for his daughter?

∽ ACT TWO ∽

▨ Puck possesses the magic flower that has the power to make someone fall in love with the first person he or she sees. What would you do with such a flower? Write the different ways you could use this flower for fun, pranks, or to heal broken hearts. Choose one scenario and write a dialogue between the lover and the recipient.

▨ "Be it cat, or bear, or boar with bristled hair . . . wake when something vile is near." These words are spoken by Oberon out of spite and jealousy as he places the "love potion" on Titania's eyelids. How do you feel about Oberon playing this trick to get what he wants? Have you ever tried to manipulate someone to get what you wanted? How did you feel, and what were the consequences of your actions?

▨ Pretend you are one of the fairies attending to Titania's sleep. Write a lullaby for the queen using images from nature that are soft, soothing, and serene. Include metaphors and similes that complement your wooded surroundings. Remember, you must impress the queen!

▨ Oberon plans for Demetrius to fall in love with Helena, but it is Lysander who awakens bewitched. We've all had experiences where something we planned didn't work out how we wanted. While Oberon had the magic flower to remedy his situation, real life doesn't offer such simple solutions. Write about a time when something didn't work out for you as planned. What caused your plans to fail? Did things eventually turn out better or worse? Looking back, is there another plan of action you could have taken? If you had the magic flower to fix your situation, how would you have used it?

▨ Though it is clear Demetrius loves Hermia and not Helena, Helena continues to pursue him. Even after Demetrius tells Helena he will leave her alone in the woods "at the mercy of the wild beasts," she still follows him. Human nature sometimes makes us want things we can't have. Why do you think not being able to have something makes it more desirable?

✂ ACT THREE ✂

▦ Puck joyously turns Bottom into a creature with the head of an ass. If you had the power to turn people into creatures, animals, or plants, how would you use it? Who would you change, and into what would you change him or her? Write a short fictional account of one magical change you would make and its comical consequences.

▦ There are many, many stories and fairy tales of a "beauty" falling in love with a handsome prince, but there are fewer about a "beauty" falling in love with a "beast," like Titania and Bottom. Compare and contrast the first type of story to the second. Though Titania is meant to look silly by falling in love with the "lowly" mortal, is there a message in this that goes beyond the comic element? If so, what do you think that message is?

▦ Titania falls hopelessly in love with Bottom after Oberon places the flower juice on her eyelids. What would happen if Oberon refused to release Titania from the spell, or if he lost the flower and couldn't change her new love interest? Write what might happen between Titania and Bottom if their love endured. Would they marry? What difficulties might they face? Would they be accepted among the fairies?

▦ Hermia feels great anguish and jealousy because Lysander suddenly proclaims his love for Helena. Write about a time you felt jealous over a friend's or family member's attention. What makes people jealous? What are the best ways to deal with jealous feelings?

▦ In order to decide who gets to be with Helena, Demetrius and Lysander challenge each other to a duel. Do you think this is a logical way to make a decision? What are its advantages? disadvantages? What other ways could they have come to a decision? Demetrius and Lysander never stop to ask Helena whom she prefers. What does this say about the status of women in Athenian society?

⌘ ACT FOUR ⌘

▨ Oberon decides to repair the "mistakes" he and Puck made with the magic flower. If you had a magic flower that could correct the problems of the world, what would you fix? Discuss two or three changes you would make and how they would affect society.

▨ Lysander and Hermia disobey Athenian law by running away to get married. Is it ever okay to break the law? If so, under what circumstances? Were Lysander and Hermia justified in their actions? If you were a judge, would you convict them? Why or why not?

▨ Egeus is very angry with his daughter for disobeying him. Think about and write down his reasons for being angry, and then discuss whether these reasons are justified. How did the status of women during this period in Athens affect the course of women's lives? How might the father/daughter relationship be different today?

▨ When Titania refuses to give Oberon the Indian child, Oberon manipulates her in order to get his own way, and places her in an awkward, embarrassing situation. List several compromises and/or solutions Titania and Oberon could develop to solve their dilemma.

▨ In all respects, Titania and Bottom are opposites. Bottom is a common, uneducated Athenian citizen, and Titania is a beautiful fairy queen, capable of supernatural powers. Yet, because of the magic flower, Titania falls in love with Bottom. Do you believe that opposites attract, or do you think people who fall in love are very similar? Which type of relationship do you think is better? more exciting? comfortable? Which might last longer?

∞ ACT FIVE ∞

The "actors" in the play *The Most Lamentable Comedy, and Most Cruel Death of Pyramus and Thisby* are extremely nervous about performing for the duke and duchess. Write about a time you had to perform or speak in front of an audience. How did it feel to be in front of a crowd? Is there a "secret" you can share that could help others cope with this situation?

Of the three marriages that take place at the end of the play, which do you see as being the most stable? Why? Considering the events and dialogue between these characters in the story, list the positive and negative qualities of all three future marriages.

It is obvious throughout the play that *Pyramus and Thisby* will be a hilarious, amateurish production. Write a review of the worst movie, TV show, or book you have seen or read. Discuss the characters, situations, and settings, and how they contributed to making the story so disappointing. When finished, share your review with the class. Do any of your classmates share your opinion?

Write a dialogue of the cast of *Pyramus and Thisby* after they perform their play and are on their way home from the palace. Will their interpretation of the play's success be different from that of the duke and duchess? What will each character say about his or her individual performance?

The wedding guests make fun of the play *Pyramus and Thisby* because it is melodramatic and ridiculous, yet the "lovers" in the play aren't much more ridiculous than those in the audience. Referring back to particular events in the story, discuss which lovers appear the funniest and why. Why do you think love makes people do funny, outrageous things?

ALL THE WORLD'S A READERS' THEATER

You may wish to perform the play as a readers' theater rather than a full production. This technique allows students to participate with little preparation. You can even assign two or three students to one role. Make sure students have thoroughly reviewed the play and their lines before performing. Even though this will be an informal performance, encourage students to wear costumes and stand or walk around when their characters are speaking.

IMPROMPTU PERFORMANCES

After reading and discussing the summary of the play, divide the class into seven or eight groups and distribute a summary to each. Have groups decide where they think the summary should be broken down into scenes. Depending on your class size, have groups each take responsibility for performing one or two scenes for the class. Invite groups to perform using their own interpretation and language. Students will enjoy using their own "lingo," and you will be amazed to see the play come to life with students' own words and emotions.

Before groups perform, have them write a short summary of the scenes for which they are responsible. For example:

Scene One—Egeus brings his daughter Hermia to the duke so she will follow Athenian law and obey him by marrying Demetrius. Hermia claims to love Lysander, but the duke tells her she must obey her father, live in a nunnery, or be put to death. Lysander then tells Hermia of a plan for their escape.

Scene Two—Lysander and Hermia tell Helena of their plan to leave Athens and marry in secret. Helena decides to tell Demetrius in hopes he will love her for it.

Scene Three—The actors, led by Peter Quince, are assigned roles for the upcoming play they will perform at the duke's wedding.

Scene Four—In the wood, Puck and a fairy discuss the argument between their king and queen, Oberon and Titania. Oberon is jealous and wants to take an Indian boy from Titania to use as his servant.

Scene Five—Oberon and Titania meet in the wood and argue about the Indian boy. Titania refuses to give him up and leaves. Oberon tells Puck to obtain a magic flower with which he can play a trick on Titania.

REBUILDING THE GLOBE

Invite student groups to construct small versions of the Globe Theatre. They can use boxes, cardboard tubes, tagboard, fabric and wrapping-paper scraps, yarn, and various other art supplies. Make sure they refer to an accurate picture of the Globe and include the many special attributes of Shakespeare's stage, including trapdoors that fall into "hell" and a canopy above the stage as "heaven." Encourage students to be creative and add actors onstage as well as patrons in the audience. Invite students to display their creations. As an extension, invite groups to "act out" a scene from the play using their theatres, and characters made from cardboard, spools, or even sock puppets, depending on the size of the models.

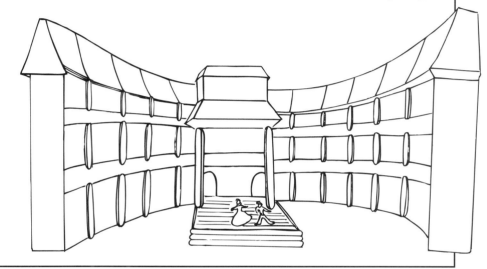

ALAKAZAM! YOU'RE SHAKESPEARE!

Invite students to write "Shakespeare style." Divide the class into groups of four or five, and have each group choose a short passage from a favorite story or play. Have students rewrite the chosen passage imitating Shakespeare's beautiful prose and verse. Provide each group with a list of common words found in Shakespeare's work, such as *doth, hither, thee, wilt, fair, bid, adieu,* and so on. Have volunteers type passages into a computer, using special fonts and designs. Invite students to illustrate the designed pages, and then bind them into a class book.

DETAILS, DETAILS

The details of the plot in *A Midsummer Night's Dream* are important for students to understand and follow the story. Read the summary aloud, and encourage students to pay particular attention to the characters' motives and how the "play within a play" of *Pyramus and Thisby* fits into the overall picture. On chart paper, draw a concept map or flow chart of each scene to place the complex series of events into a simplified form.

MUSIC, MAESTRO!

Many works of classical music are based on Shakespeare's plays. Felix Mendelssohn wrote "A Midsummer Night's Dream," which is based on Shakespeare's play. Obtain a recording of Mendelssohn's "A Midsummer Night's Dream," and play it for your students. Ask students to close their eyes as they listen and see if they can interpret "voices" from the play, including music relating to specific scenes and/or characters.

GETTING AROUND THE WOODS

In *A Midsummer Night's Dream*, characters pop quickly in and out of scenes, searching, following, lost, and dreaming. To help keep these characters "in order," have each student choose a character to "follow" throughout the play on a map. Have students draw maps of the enchanted wood and create a "character trail" for their chosen characters. Starting at the beginning of the story, have students show the paths their characters take, using symbols to represent various places their characters sleep, argue, woo, and so on. Have students include detailed keys to show what these symbols mean.

FLOWER FOR SALE!

Invite student groups to create ad campaigns for Oberon's magic flower, the Love-in-idleness. They must come up with a pitch, slogan, and one unique way to market to their target audience. Who would be most likely to buy such a flower? What would be the best ways to reach this audience—radio, television, direct mail, billboards, magazines, newspapers, or skywriting? Would getting testimonials from several "satisfied customers" be effective? Ask students to create their campaigns around one of these ideas and present them to the class. Give awards for Most Creative, Most Clever Copy, Best Acting (for a commercial), Most Artistic, and so on.

TRAVEL BROCHURE

Have students create travel brochures for the forest of the fairies. Before they begin, provide sample travel brochures as examples. Invite students to include "photos" (drawn or cut from magazines) and descriptive copy, including opportunities for outings, special features, modes of transportation, places to stay, and so on. Students can design their brochures for either humans (mortals) or fairies as visitors.

MY SPECIAL VALENTINE

Have student pairs make valentines from two of the play's lovers. Have each pair make valentines for both a female and male character, writing as they would write to the one he or she loves. When finished, have pairs exchange valentines and write back to the card's author in the guise of the addressee. For example, "Helena" could try to persuade Demetrius to love her, and "Demetrius" could tell her he is in love with someone else.

DAYDREAMS OR NIGHTDREAMS?

Create a large Venn diagram on the chalkboard to compare and contrast daydreams and night dreams. Label one circle *Daydreams* and the other *Night Dreams.* Being both general (how daydreams and night dreams are different) and specific (giving specific examples of dreams they have had), have students brainstorm ideas and experiences for the diagram. In the middle section, write how these two kinds of dreams are alike. Ask students, *Have you had similar day- and night dreams? What were they? How does it feel to "dream" when you're wide awake?*

SCENE TITLES

Have students write titles for each act and/or scene in the play. For example, Act One could be titled *Hermia and Lysander Plan Their Escape;* Act One, Scene One *Hermia Must Choose;* and Act One, Scene Two *The Actors Take Their Parts.* Creating titles encourages students to analyze and summarize the story in individual parts and as a whole.

WANTED!

Invite students to created a "wanted" poster for Puck, the mischievous sprite. Have them include an illustrated "photo," list of his criminal activities (mischief-making), physical description, aliases, where he was last seen, his probable whereabouts, and any rewards being offered. Discuss with students who in the play might want to capture Puck to keep him from making further mischief. What punishment might he receive if he were captured? Or might this person want to use Puck as Oberon did to spread his or her own sort of mischief?

WHAT THE POTION SET IN MOTION

For thousands of years, people have been searching for a love potion that really works. Have students invent a recipe that might make a good love potion (for example, *one cup rose petals, two tablespoons tears, three candy hearts, and one drop perfume*). Students can also create a love potion with emotions and/or attributes (for example, *two teaspoons happiness, one tablespoon loyalty, one teaspoon laughter, and a pinch of sweetness*). Invite students to present their "potions" to the class, describing their reasons for including each ingredient as well as how they would test their creations!

WHO'S IN LOVE WITH THE BEAST?

Divide the class into groups of five. Have one student in each group write a descriptive sentence about an imaginary "beast." He or she then passes the paper to the student on his or her left. This student adds one more descriptive sentence about the beast, and passes the paper to the next student, and so on. Keep papers going around the circles until each student has written two to three sentences. Have each group read about their beast to the class, and ask them to choose the "best beast."

The next day, bring in an envelope containing several pictures of movie stars, singers, athletes, models, and so on. Invite a volunteer to choose a picture and show it to the rest of the class. Tell students that a magic spell was cast upon this "star," and he or she is now in love with the beast! Have students write short stories about what happens next with these two lovers. This is an excellent jumping-off point for the story line of Bottom and Titania.

CHARACTER INTERVIEWS

Discuss with the class what constitutes a good interview, such as those on TV talk shows and the news. Divide the class into groups and assign each group a character from the play. Invite groups to write interesting interview questions to ask their characters for a class "TV talk show." Invite several volunteers to act as talk-show hosts and characters from the play on a panel for the show. Invite "hosts" to ask the characters questions generated by the class. Other class members can act as the audience, asking questions, cheering, booing, and so on. This is an excellent way to review the play, and students will love it!

THE TRAGIC DEATH OF PYRAMUS AND THISBY

To help students understand the "play within a play" story line, have them make playbills for *The Most Lamentable Comedy, and Most Cruel Death of Pyramus and Thisby*. Encourage students to design playbills as would Bottom and his cohorts, choosing text and pictures appropriate for their point of view and experience. Have students list characters in the play (perhaps adding next to Lion and Pyramus that they are only actors in a play, and patrons need not be afraid), a plot summary, actor bios and pictures, and add a colorful cover. If students perform *A Midsummer Night's Dream*, they can pass out these playbills as a humorous addition to a regular program.

ATHENS, THE REAL STORY

Shakespeare was fascinated with the world of the ancient Greeks, and wrote several plays set in this time and place. Divide the class into groups, and assign each group one topic about life in Athens during this classical period (women's and men's roles in society, entertainment, sports, art, government, and so on). Invite students to present what they learn to the class, and discuss how life in Athens compares to life today. As an extension, have groups research one topic about Athens and Elizabethan England. Invite students to discuss how life in Athens compared to life during Shakespeare's time.

A MIDSUMMER NIGHT'S DREAM REVIEW

Show students several examples of newspaper movie reviews and discuss the style in which they are written. Then invite students to write reviews of the play following these directions.

1. Attach a real (or drawn) picture of yourself to a piece of paper, and write your name, grade, and school.

2. Begin your review with one descriptive word such as *boring, exciting,* or *funny.* Write a brief review of the play, including supporting reasons why you chose that particular word.

3. Explain what you believe to be the best and worst aspects of the play.

4. Choose a character you like and one you dislike. Give reasons for your choices and how these characters affected you.

5. Give the play a grade such as A—*Outstanding,* B—*Good,* C—*Okay,* D—*A bomb!*

RENAISSANCE FEAST

To close your study of the play, celebrate with a Renaissance Feast! Have student groups research the time period (Elizabethan England) in which the play was written via the Internet or the library. Topics can include food, sports and games, clothing, music, entertainment, and so on. Invite each group to share what they learned with the class, and use the information to plan a feast. They may dress up in period clothing, prepare special foods to eat, play games, and listen to period music. You may invite parents and/or another class to your feast so students can share what they learned.

References

Coxwell, Margaret J. "Shakespeare for Elementary Students," *Teaching PreK–8* 27, no. 8 (March 1997): 40–42.

Epstein, Norrie. *The Friendly Shakespeare.* New York: Viking, 1993.

The Illustrated Stratford Shakespeare. London: Chancellor Press, 1982.

Onions, C. T. *A Shakespeare Glossary.* New York: Oxford University Press, 1986.